Wandering On Course

(Would Be Wands)

Robert Podgurski

SPUYTEN DUYVIL
New York City

Many of these poems contained in this collection first appeared in
Notus New Writing, Sulfur, Compound Eye, Open Space Magazine,
and House Organ.

ISBN 978-0-9661242-2-4

Library of Congress Cataloging-in-Publication Data

Podgurski, Robert.
  [Poems. Selections]
  Wandering on course (would be wands) / Robert Podgurski.
     pages cm
  ISBN978-0-9661242-2-4
  I. Title.
  PS3616.O288A6 2014
  811'.6--dc23
                              2013024433

Contents

III

I

Jimson's Gift

Smelling the wet peatness
Of the jungle growth of petunias
Astride the patio
Sends my mind to a less arid land
, One where lush vegetation thrives, ... feral
Chaotic growth patterns
Whose origin,
One may only speculate
On a concise
Fertile plant fetus encased
Babe in a seed opening
Cadence of hortum fecundum

Expansion of roots, wild underbrush
Gnarly brambles goetically abrading
The ground, the soft enhanced
By the nettled sting
Over in a barren corner
Datura, a lone thornapple spreads
Its limbs and toothed fronds
Alone purveying the alien unearthliness
Some things possess
So much in contact with terrum
Clue at a source beyond
The black that nestles stars.

Spiderplant

Spider
Calls herself
Clephus
She has been
With me
For years
My favorite
Arachnidafoliage
As deep rooted
Sic Cthulhu
Not sleeping
And about

Oyster Gem

Tear open to get to the mind stuff
Crudest form, but perfected shucking
Yields the golden food undisturbed,
Still
Smell Sea Brine high,
Feeling the breakers against
Back muscle nerves.

Poems of Beechnut is a Food

I
Bands of softened solar glow cut silk-swift
rustling and twisting thru trees.
The wind took on the appearance of a strange bird race
close to being reptilian
                             in feel but not looks
      Wisps — the nephews of gusts
crept in, between the boards of our study to form the long
      slender lines in russet orange swirl that led
      to the eagle-like head.
    Imparting only to me a sense
        that death had not come
        even though it felt that way.

II

That there is pain in the field
where the brush, reeds & hedgerows have been cropped
, sheared down
      yielding enmity
            and
                  Growing energy where previously red-
                  winged blackbirds could perch
                  and run sentries.
      Taking no further,
      cut off the haven and the potential to metaphor.
      For we cannot gather the plants
      transformed to violence by the harvest
      technique, i.e., rendered usable.
      In other words, let the clearing come back
      & the rushes lay upon our mind.
                  For a fitting crown
                  the hat that is a hut
                  radiant compost heat.

III

Beechnut—the eternal
   try–not
     pods

  I remember picking up from the grounds
  of Bushy-Run Battlefield in my youngest years
  –Also Blevins' stepping-stone into the court
  of the half-kings Guyasuta & Gaustarax.

       Resemble star anise
  scent a much more subtle arrow-matique flavor.
  Four wooden petals expand as they dry
  blossom to expose two tri-form seeds   6 in 4 Lotus power.
  Nut as Meat.
  But as Greene's Friar Bacon admonished
 "To let thee see how scholars use to feed
 How little meat refines our English wits"

Yet magicians are the true chefs and ingredients of the convivium
    of sense the woody food cast from the tree.
    Tough mind-stuff
    & tough mind-stuffers.
      Together circle a cycle into
      intent's golden orb.

IV

<u>Earth</u>

<u>of Water</u>   An apple clear ripening
on the verge of autumn moonlight
      eves & wisps of dark cold salubrious air.
For biting into, clearing out the summer heat and wind
helps to round out the meditation
      On <u>fire</u> beech-nut symmetry
     it is the sex of the symbol that drives us wild
      snapping a sharp invagination
      on seed blades, bouncing off rays   so
         the sight
         beams wild.
            Building a bridge between
           oculus   &   intellectus
The fecund bed of the phantasm.

– The Poet is the page, nature writes on –

V

His back
A servant & courier of the ever-widening rift
where to plant it.
As Joachim Tanckius felt,
    whether it be vegetable, mineral, or animal seed
the plot, or womb is crucial for it draws
from the *mumia* the ground exudes; like produces like.
        The babe in the egg is a mummy
        and its perfection can only be found
        in   resurrection birth
Balsam
        No further.

VI

The turf I drum with my feet
    kicks up a rhythm of mixed fruits.
Some acidic and sour
     others mellowed sweet like rotted apples.
               Give off a musk
             in the air of tanninsence.

            Fall temple.

    The poet cannot help
    but become the things
    written about.
Harvest frozen in the dry form
    of the nut anchored in its static bloom
        Wired for security
         for life
            propagation
    Cured it can be dropped

           Will—not—break.

               9/12/94–10/5/94

To the Whore
of
Singing Hounds

My friends can be found
rooting through briars and thorns of obscure ground.
They run forest floors, gamboling,

                         twisting

                             , and gyrating
At grinding slow speeds.

   Labyrinthine convolutions
      protecting small patches of ground from traffic
         seldom trodden tracts,
          tractatus de orba sacra   read off the stripped
                                   bark of trees.
Without clearing
through dull blackened green undergrowths,
nettle numbed perspectives
         in syn-anesthesia
from their hell-gates' harrowed sleep.

Goetic garlands of brier thorn and bracken
span the coarse nape of my scaly
Goddess takes pleasure from special scrapes
a throat that swallows wayward angst and tension.
        Wraps her spit around
        notes that split the sullen
        inattentive ear
        on a moment's sudden hearing.

Judge,
      jury,
            and witness
                        all beheaded
         For lascivious treats
         tryst for eternity.

Sipping bitter aperitifs
grip base of the soul
by route of throat.

Let it be a gentle reminder
her claws can't be made
into an ornament for show
and worn as she bears
all claimed for her own.

                     1/4/98

Fall in Love with the Brave

I
Collapsed Blue Bird house.
        Mournful instinct
                insures the parent's non-return
to the young dying as they must
upsets me far more greatly
than I could have guessed.
The home I erected
fallen now their grave.

II
At the escarpment's summit
a snarling hellhound greeted
and prevented our descent
                strange? Ironic?
only to depart after its most vicious display.

& the perfectly desiccated possum's corpse
fur, brown from decay
highlights white exposed ribs opened cage
having long ago let loose its life.

& the peregrine falcon
chasing off the turkey buzzard
                south
—something about hell I thought

and stars,
      a conflict
          or just a dance
    changing places.

III
So I listen to the silent connections
        without a sound
absorbing as much as possible
point toward dark nested hopes
          infinity
      ever

an expanding haven

Frog, Wind, and somewhere
a Snake

Following the laid song lines
our Cockatiel, Puck, has shown me
the search   of seeking where a voice
sounds best and is drawn from
such as beneath the boulders
or riding some current over tree tops.

Sonic shows on filial lineaments
gripped from the depths like some
green goddess clawing at the back of brains
her tunneling voice, a rock drill to enter.
Owls do it, they emerge and resuscitate
some inner clutch to divide & disperse
in the soul circulatory routes of blood,

                            and burning.

Tumbling voices down the hill
and the auctioneers roll the figures off their tongues
back up to the crags on Dixon School road.
Their echoes acrobatic bouncing I catch
the crossing with my ears,
but turn
our noise to others' ways & make them stop,
yet do they listen and to what?
Some sirens fear that distractions
won't prove fatal or at least life
changing but never spare sense,
this echo's a trickster on the fade.

Creatures in dreams, beasts
a bear become wart hog
with a bone in its forehead turns into an eye,
I ask, "are you friendly" and it replies "no!"
as it makes me feel good and lets me by
taking direction
by sound of frog, wind, and a pattern
rosy quartz and grey green beads
I know,
        unnamed,
                a snake
                        that's most evasive to the ear

Demon Teeth

              One by one they get stuck in the scalp

I need to go north
needing to winter

              drops of perspiration replaced by beads of blood.

A heavily ozonated haze
is unbreathable
and the chiggers are a drag.

              following the dotted line about the scalp

gone south for the summer
into some abandoned ring of hell

                 fangs sink for the tear off,
                 sever cranial sutures
                 and open a new mind.

    Is the shaft
    hounds of hell avoid
    for worming thought
    matter to wrestle itself under
    gut fruit guano in
    the heaven of the mole
    & playground for the grub.

    Even when you've hit rock bottom
    there is still lower to go
    into the malign gyre
    of 'ol soft shoe shufflin' black end soul.

Omen Pentecost

"Bene vixit, qui bene latuit"

Ovid

Make fire and they will come
Before building.
The salamander shows   in the fire pit.
With surrounding surprise beyond the containment
Of the stone circle we descried

                                        Slime covered

          An unlikely creature of fire

                                        Hides

          As the starter caught

                                        Or just returns

          To its mother tongue

                              Flame lapped

                                        Source of Life.

II

And what it meant
                    Before
                                   The Walking Stick
                         Blues conflated expedition.
               Kicking up sparks like Artaud's cane
The stick walked up by our congregation
Spelling out his condition
                    and evoking our response

Through the signal of its sigils
             Traced by a dance upon the earth
                     Camouflaged
                             Hiding amongst
                                     Fallen twigs
                                             and would-be wands.

To search for one here
Is to hazard a special fatigue,
        Delirium.
Instead, let it plod from out of the talus,
Find your preoccupied gaze.
                             Seized,
As I extended my finger in greeting
Touched its leg,
                locked in fascination
                             in West Virginia
Is a seal set free of fate
Left gone to the atavistic
Happenstance reinforcement,
                Conjuration of serpent wonder.

                             Why there could be a need to search
                             for reminders is insane.

III

Like hiking Hart Crane country, Ohio
Or even living there.
Walking, like the stick
concealed amongst all the failing branches
Bending with the wind,
                              cloaking inner weaknesses.
But soul-giving movement,
                    A re-animator
                    Of lost up-stream swimmers
                    Spawning thrusts against the current
                    Eggs all on.

Beat and fried,
now content to find in the underbrush
Tensile strength and flexibility
—Those elusive devil gems,   a double treat—
In absentia,
        Incognito
                Cognition.

                    New River Gorge, West Virginia—Gates Mills, Ohio
                    11/3/96

Wings of Judgment

> "And your wings
>> Disturbing the Exact Harmony of the stars"
>>> Denis Devlin

Trillium splayed whiteness on the forest floors
As the vultures cruise thermals on a Saturnian course.
Cathartes aura—Cleansers of the air over the crags
They're said to return to Hinckly, Ohio each March 15th.
The truth is they never leave

At night congregating in roosts,
No nests but in crags
The climber's credo.

Once known as Ossifrages, bone crushers
Land or hover about places where bloody massacres may happen.
Generals would watch their patterns before battle.

Clouds of judgment gather beneath the hungry circle
Hovering for a slow death
Prepared feast
To open up a wake.

Accompanied by the cavernous unholy O of the Owl
Hunting at night in the Gorge
Speaking to me in ravenous intonations.
I must start to listen, abandon the pen and absorb
Or let unfounded promises prey
And indolence charm.

Hungry night eye
Formidable,

        Fed

           Keeps its luster concealed
           Veiled to day.

Filling the Ossuaries with blind tongue fire
Many pick up in our marrow hunting down
Auguries we tote sacrificial messages to our fellow's
Imagination's pyre, will that bones speak.

In the passive act of reading their fragments
Like leftover graffiti set in the earth's frame
Framed the wings on the scarab fossil
That belonged to the magical child in the dream paper thin
and delicate just barely petrified.
A large beetle-like creature camouflaging itself against
The fossil got up and tried to crawl away unnoticed
As I focused on the wings set in dark green.

Those Griffon Vulture's wings of judgment,
The Egyptians called Maati
For justice is either fleeting
Or it relies on carnage
And is just adjustment
Imbibing remains.

Impressed on the solitary orb
The dove that glanced off my car's fender
Somersaulted landing behind me
Wing outstretched image, can't forget
Giving scavengers gifts.

Framework picked clean the old bag of bones
No longer needs its bag, that kenning's stripped down
A device de-viced
                    Of hungry flesh
Fetching
        Bones are the stellar groundwork that gives
Us a leg and a form to stand on,
                              Removed,
                      We spread out into a sea.

                                    5/13/97-6/13/97

Root Extraction

The study of the exhumed
veins the meat of the earth
blood as it appears inside
can never be seen so are tendril beds

Terrestrial pages are provided
by a gaze
        surface rendering
such sap drawn from a tree till none's left
this violence may appear gentle at a glance

Secretive undulating patterns
spread out so much that they may be
film-like in their ability to cover
a bullsnake's molted skin on the south side
of the dome boulder above Dixon School Road.

Wind wraps around the swirling rhododendron boughs
along King's Pinnacle Ridge
on the western side half torn up exposed
roots never seen in the sun
        that can only be felt by a moonless night
          or so the primitive notion goes
on under wildly
        preventing writing during the thrall
later to re-collect and interpret as dust collects
such is the way of ancient sight,

working on and through
still moments
motions to adjourn

in the natural court
just doesn't work, (but abjures the need of labor)

Worm and snail trail convulsion / convolution.

Walking Cherokee Covered Lands

At the South Fork Pisgah Wilderness are

waking up at camp

        I saw a hinged sign

    Do

    Not

    Leave

    ———

    Weave

for the unbelievers below stating "Do Not Enter"

and so we gravitated to that spot.

Eye cast net over everything

on an expanding basis

    the whole

        not quite separated by a crystalline membrane

          and in its limited focus alone

            obfuscating

backed by the all absorbing blackness

the visions had

On the ridge line

converging, choreographing

nostalgic urges

want of an expanded view

and the push

beneath what is now called

Pilot Knob.

John said the Cherokee thunder god, Kunnati / red man

resided on the nearby mountain

little is said of him,

and that's reasonable as he has made himself

heard enough

across sky /   attendant ears

beneath the ground a different story's concealed

noticing what trees leave behind

root over rock,—a driven overlay (splitting force)

typically hidden lattice shows.

On Copper Ridge Bald

the dialectic with the Raven Mocker

            was pregnant with John watching

we heard answers to glowing minerals' intent

and stag-horn lichen pullulating

            coaxed by wind whisp(ers

Succubi sentries at Burning Town Gap Road

camp   desires kept in check

the vision crept upon higher lines,   evoked.

Heading back to civilization   /   surrounding and its noise

memories in our bones / muscles

supporting against the quotidian pressures

Relieved, relived in steps.

Smoldering Reason

Get a read on a character's embers
by the wind given
their life.
Such glow exists by virtue of exhalation
order ordained and set inexorably
frozen in place
vulcanized first.

                Having walked past a stone on the Western Way
                with slashes, cracks and pockets seemed to exhibit
                a naturally occurring form of Ogham
                and it appeared that some early Celts
                who divined by rocks reading them
                said to themselves, maybe this is a good
                text formed by sun fire and time's ice
                acutely etched worthy of emulation.

Burning curmudgeonly peat,
hard to start without coal
but together are incense of bog and heath
low flames but with warming strength
grown out of the decayed relationship
of the plant, walk, and feather fallen in layers.
And the wind that smooths over the bodies
that shakes the barley
, combs the plain.

An almost diseased yellow vapor
appears to arise from the infernal genie,

                              perique
by itself a tobacco of miasmic power
suffumigates with depth
no wonder Crowley always had to have a supply,
caustic, "with little left but pipe and wit"…
only grown in the Bayou
first prepared in a press by the Choktow Indians
under a tree stump lever pressed for one year
fermenting into a silky blackness
giving way to the chthonic godless seepage of the swamp
it burns a mist, viscous.

Gaulloises, can clear an entire corner of a bar
even one occupied by ardent smokers
the most miasmic cigarette ever manufactured
Joel Oppenheimer still had to have 'em
with one lung his was the casual precision
burning by a babe, undulating wisps
carefully touched.
The (t)issue then comes down to burn
or be burnt
by proximity to the source some lights just torch brighter.

So their time is limited
by numbered breaths
each one an extension of truth
that the light has a source but darkness,
                              just is
and is the haven of returns
no deposits accepted
                              just reclamations

On Skin of the art that makes
pure and impure
                    intentions
                          animate enough to carry on
                                as a shadow does after the dancer stops
abruptly.
            The remainder cannot but help follow momentum
after all, the fallen in battle may re-cycle without knowing
what they were fighting about

luminosities that glow with each breath
points of intersection — reactions occur
Tesla coiled temperaments
align the self with the electric hive-wire webs jolting out past security
toward a communal strength / personal vulnerability
committing potent(see)s.

Lightning explosions

Fire crackers.

Certain people are coded,
some lettered, loaded,
others without a need their life such a script
a poem rare and hammered out
being the best and often the most difficult
are the ones worth working for.

May 2007
From Connemara, Ireland to North Carolina

The Moors

Driving, we bumped and lurched down the hill into
The path into Livermore   cemetery

        Lifted a   3 crows   Shot 22
     Fallen gravestone.   Shells at
      From the side of   Old dead
     The hill and sat it   Branches
        Back up

        The current of
       Deep, deep old ones
        Is not a lingering
         Thing of the
          Past
           There
         Elements act up
          Drawing
            In
         From below
         Draw down
         Intermingle
       And exchange
          Giving
           Back
          Energy

Livermoor, Liver-dale, resembling a corner of Scotland.
Swampy land and receded water as viewed from atop
The viaduct stone-4 in all with an old city washed away
                                    remains under water.

The appropriate spot at the end of a highway 982, turning into a dirt path
gently descends into a cove trees guard and loom over up to the gate, the
entrance to a graveyard, hunched and falling over the hill. A stone dated
1789 no loner stands that I viewed on my early visits there. Can't even
get in the back way. They watch it these days. The moor looks better now.

                                        People still do
                                        Evil things on
                                            Hilltops
                                        Late at night.
                                        Hidden out
                                            of view
                                            in parts.

            Legba is on the lookout
            at this spot no wrong
            Hoodoo goin' down here.

3rd trestle and remembering. The spot
Those who seek ones who see
Get a peek this place
The other side
Most hide from
By ignoring

   Supports   Alone in   Without   These   Remnants
   Symmetric   Black water   Bridge   To support   Remaining

               The five sided block
               Is shattered that ecclesiastics
               Stand behind, because
               Fear.

This is an area
For `crying unto
The hills'
   And silencing
The frogs   Idiot flutists
                               Jamming

A few

                  Wild dogs

Luna Thoughts

(for Butch Kunkle)

Passed thru
The River issued the command
     –Order, no more–
False images & messages from the brain to the body
jam on the one-way response ramp
out of the dictator's rule
     to a magical fascism.
  Dialectical levers disarmed
  pseudo-language discourses abandoned
for plain signs incited by love
etched in wills tougher than granite
    are what poet's quills
     running on dry beds
       inevitably resort
    To wash-outs – Desert ravines
      dry as blotting sand.
    Until rain in the high country converts
    them into raging sluices.
  Oceans teeming with mild highs
and like droplets of Mercury
    any attempt to finger quick-silver seas
only detonates the large into countless beads
        , and so on.
      Till we first sing clearly
      for ourselves
      and the bed becomes

                                    packed down
                                    unable to leach
                                    our mobility
                                    or quick witsaway.

        Just the opposite
        of Blaser's moths
      For 33 elusive years
absent.
        And then one cool mist laden
        morning
                    in the Laurel hills of my youth
        Sleeping on a cross beam at the ranger's station
        perched a Luna Moth.
        Wings heaving with the wind
        , defensive false eyes peering
                        on the same lift
        while concealed
                    pitch infinite dark orbs at rest.

Looking unreal, as all other-worldly creatures of this sort do
                    I touched his soft green tail,
                                it stirred
                        so I stopped,
                    senses reified.

        They have always been portentous
                    once and for all I had given up,
                    then it appeared.

Lesson learned
A bow is strung
and soft moon majesty uncloaks
with large feathered antennae.
Fallopian receptivity,
Subtle vibrations,
Mental insemination.

Dark chamber to tool loose
a long fought fancy.
Tagging along on black night's
dream backs,
The hinterlands
of untouched thought
It sat silent
to my amazement.

But as all this goes down
She flies,
pricked notions race
with the nascent summer.

A common white moth
I first noticed led me

on
Those that can be seen everywhere
may reveal the long sought jewels,

                    elusive youth's
                    desirous fairy.
Found,
      Released,
            and part of the trance becomes
                     an embellishment.
           In the seal
         Impressae on the hot sensuous wax
that lets the self free to wander
       and plots a course set by directions so detailed
         Precision
             is untenable
           based on all that we have learned

              till now.

              Kooser State Park
              Jones Mills Pennsylvania
                 28 June 1995

Of Whirling Air

Errant knavery
sitting at the base
of Tierrany Wall
in Obed wilderness, Tennessee
ignoring the obvious signs of her fury
                        and formation.

Lightning and distant thunder.
Evening darkness falls in seconds.
Mounting the storm.
Hail shower, a giveaway
of dark cloud's intent that rolled
down the gorge's corridor.
a coiling of *lung mei*
                        and then release
Rushing to the canyon's rim
with a sound I'll never forget
of whirling air
drowning out the rapids' thunder
as it lost the resonance of wind and rose
to an inferno's roar cracking and popping.
Air, a thousand arms twirling blades
swiftly tore
            timber
                    earth,
                            and time
                    to shreds

turned our minds
inside out upon the moment,
ecstatic voyeurs of the most primeval
beauty and rage.

That dense forest harrowed
lay a bare swatch exposed.
Freeing a field by hell
work of the true leveler—Bhavani
Kali holding the lopped off heads,
and trunks in sway.

II
Afterwards on the back way
picking up pieces of hail,
Earthed fury,
              Solid manna
by the heat of my hands fount
liquefied,
              instinctively anointing forehead and glands
this precious nectar of the hell-bound
heavens released in beads
with a humbled sub-mission
my significant otherness twirled aloft again.

II

The Hope for a C(ode
to a Parallel Uni(verse

Spheres
Ring

As when two resonant things
caught in mutual attraction
charming each other into chiming
in a toast collide.

Or when someone's finger
leaves a crystal goblet's rim
from round upon round
and the singing dissipates
such circles without circumference
radiating like tossed pebbles
do with placid pond water
spanning past finite
Souls mirror motion
spun from this creative reflex
to fade from here
                        and gradually reverberate
                              to an antipodean ear
and maybe return

Sacred volley.

Inner Sorceries Outwardly Seeking

Where I can pray to nothing
awakened 3 am on a Wednesday night
Whirlwind thrashed through the trees
howling,   trembling in its center
precipitated by a burgeoning passion.
, So the container broke, right?!
        Left letting it loose.

And rhythmically breathing back-in
        The Chinook prowled on to the east
                        Returned for a moment
                        & Moved off

                                Which I made happen

Consumed by the Volatile,
Dark woman vapors
Set my wonder to rushing airs
        and whirling fires.

In the headless, mindless thing's
Feet   Loose
When the dark glistening hole of Deepest Sleeps
Brings me
Here.

On The Lam(ia)

Do not assume
Lilith's position,
Discernible,
Times
       the many conceived
             equals
              naught.
Reigning above with sheer impunity
over this mad race
posturing not for just anything.

But penetration riding on
every molecule
       thought
       an open space
          is her wraith
          under the multitude of the sacred   whores
          only a few shine as servants   of the star
Assuming her position
pounding the patriarchy
Jigging,
    Gigging
          Wriggling off its crank
          rodent caught in her trap
          he fights to twist and tear it off
          and be like her

                        so that she
              may like him
                        be unrestricted.
Movement becomes the curvature
overture,
          spinal,
                    tactic,
Next to the sensual arch
          in the back
                              next to the air
                              that pleasurably envelopes
                              each line is the mounting
                                        exchange tantric voltage
                              stroking for sparks
                    beyond all Yuga's
                                        Yogins

II
The living/dead
          come on
people that become their drives
          simply ridden into
walking away from their tombs
          Rilke's Hectare
knew full well
          their deceased clientèle's
          souls fall with their flaccid will.

III
Time for the rite of the shuddering
        repulsion after ensnared
                in the glue of attraction

The big smile
        most importantly
        from having a talk with sex
        everyone appears to want to have
        but taking a moment to listen
        to what she has to say
without words, sensation / epidermal reveals the clothing
        sheathes the urge
wrapped about object and desire, invasion and submission
all for fleeting ecstasy, which, turned on its head between
legs and thinking there carefully before exposure
can extend and maintain the glorious
bliss,

        (side by side
        instead of

Depending on a Current

When natural pulse
exceeds a synthetic high
seething and uttering
to know things,
no things have the organs
like ours that swell with blood
yearning to exchange
between membranes
this watered show,
                              sanguine life
carefully vibrated a word arouses any one
carefully placed
with focused breath, electric stroke

Comes swimming from the night to meet me
after harassing the other would-be gaunts and lamias
where poems have wrought a raunchy bed of uncertain airs
feed the luscious effluvia that surrounds

Tasting memories,
for you,
your flavor, a clear resin, rasa,
springs defiled water
                              refreshing
cold so intense *like copper pennies on the tongue*

Glands set little fires you like
not to be put out.
in your shell shielded fishiness
selfish and coveting
running away, shorn by the cloven blade
old souls penetrated,
                laid   open

passive oysters' fetid bed
awash in a grimy tide
their irritations', our pearl, inspirations
are sisters
                times are tearing apart
         to expose art
full words,
at the base
of pregnant
feelings.

(untitled)

Above bathroom stall blistered paint
from a cigarette ember etched inscription
        KILL ME
I found some tantric wisdom:
"For a good time
call yourself
        a stranger"

it then followed,
For a binding time
Call stranger,
        yourself

or maybe just
Call yourself strange
and be with it.

A Meditation on "The Enigma"*

(For Barb)

This severe movement

                  of separation.

And nascent choosing has placed us

Ether side of the no-man's plain.

      On

       A live

       Realm of scoria

Extends on ad-infinitum.

There is no rest when your bodies

      Through your hands keep having sex

      Gushing caustic all over the irrational land

   Pallet for the mix of Tantric art-work.

        Ochre,

              daubs

      Plunge thumb down and you

      Can feel it through your smooth holes

  , Devastating !

A volcano once raged through here,

  Now

 It's gone

And the magma of her grace

                –Flows

Still–

*A painting by Gustav Dore

II

Once it has hardened,
What of the unborn and undead
    Who never had a chance
      Or too much of one
And maybe got so far as to sprout.
  But the ravaged land bereft of fertile grace
    Strangles the life out of them,
      Wranlons,
        Less fortunate than fungus
          For they can never spread.
              Re-seed.
        Devoid of succulence
  Cracks and fissures of the land's baked clay surface
    Yearn to ooze with fecund juices
But the lusting sun just fucks it dry.

  And so her body
    Potent in *potentia*
  Remains an edifice supine
Permitting only a select few
      Dwellers at the porthole
   Yearning to become
  Someone's magical wish
    At Orgasm
    A chance

III

From a glorious conjunction
On this plane of oppositions
　　Who've slaughtered each other
During the precise moment of the conflict's cessation
　　We meet on our own terms
Using our self-fashioned key to undo
　　The enslavement of wed-lock
Re-marrying every time we assume
　　The body of beasts and embrace.
Setting the field to flames,　　cleansing
　　　　When the incendiary passion becomes so great
　　Resistance in turn becomes futile
　　　　　And that very agonizing moment
　　　　　　Between reaching out and touching
　　　　　　Threatens the order of our entire universe.

Then it's gone.

Translation's Host

(for Peteris)

"O gold, stray but alive / on the dead ash of our hearth"
From H.D. "The Tribute"

Burning, the after-smell
pure charcoal fumes in the storage room
& memory of old cordite from spent .45 shells
minds me   you are
there of a capacity
memory store
lodged against the sea and   time
                            you cannot understand
                            while immersed in it.

At last to leave & comprehend

back and forth waiting
for the coals to whiten for the organic
                            fowl dinner
Barb and I will eat,
                      the searing scent
      , strong butts & your way
        in the air on each leg
                      the process assuring me.

Now the flesh
begins to cook, soon,
                does the soul
                        become food
        if you were here
        you would be fed too
        but at a distance
        it must be different

between agape and eros
invokes suffering
having violated the boundary
separating them by necessity
            bleeding the cup dry
            and emptying the heart
            true love at rest
   & agitation
saying it is
somehow not the same.

A Twilit Sufi Tribute

Travels in images' roots searching
fine hair spread convolutions
fibrous anchored tresses,
tangles with a purpose for the whole.
                              But not moving topsoil
beneath a fermenting sea of leaves.
The moldering mass extends a hand
                     You take it
before it takes you away
as pagan brambles' food
the garden once fertilized upon a time
                        by your dreams
& together go feral.
That hieroglyph will never lend
itself to interpretation,
the change it embraces is constant
in designs of tellurian undertow.

II
In the wash of desires
there is a grey part of the mind
                     I do not go to
where matter of ambition, goals,
                              direction
are dissolved
                & the line of distinction fades
I slide off of

down the eroding bank
of trusts a loose bed of sand
Archimedes couldn't stand
on to consider faith nor force.
I do not go there out of choice but time outside of time,
                              down time,
                    will have its sway.
Eventually cascade into the shoal,
                         parched skeletal remnants
                 not quite stagnant water gnaws away
         at each grain   this world sets up and sits on.
Realm of submission
                    on the edge, the hell it takes
                    wading in with the undead and in-between
                    souls yearning
                              in the pool of the past
                         devouring saliva where all are reduced.
Remains leave a temporary message here on the slimy floor,
charnel and flecks of the star-born greedily sucked down,
On the edge it makes no sense,
                              but once in I'm over my head-
                                        less-ness.

III

Up-rising from sea beds
Fog kings, emperors between sky, land, and water
would rhyme with dogs in Sirius games
but can't and only bow on their way to conquer
time with misty blanket space,
the earth objects disappear,
and leave the eye to wakeup
scenes and phantasy-scapes
from barely made out things.

Wandering royally
those who venture
this vague realm
ready-to-be molded
and construed in a play-
ful unknowing that breeds
      cultures sublime
are the Dionysian spores
that make drunk
Wine of this holy erosion.

The Pool of Flesh
and
The Holy Sea

In still waters of reflection
  edge of icy mind
          thru meditation // Post-Orgasmic calm
stretching bliss out on waves.
Ananda the song, we are the notes
the great being keeps on pulling.
Flesh pools quench wayward thoughts in
a fluid ardent vive eruption
from spermatozoal flight to egg
flesh arises from a holy sea.

Aqua-felt
Being from the start
Birth blood, the testament—amniotic 1st sign of emergence
the water breaks
rising, sun as power comes thru days
Gate of the sea-goat's horns.

A snake that rooted in the depths rises
from out the viscera-tunnels, writhes and swims
the fork, the double edge fused by the ecstasy, tongue
activator of an hollow reed
unholy, the stop put to the pipes.

Our water devil.

What is the flesh
purpose of all works.

The air a thickened glaze
and voices form clothed in sects
dripping tongues from mouthing what they're not
without rules thoughts in garments lacking careful measurements
Create Golem trysts where fancies rule
in true desires' stead
and eat their words to subdue.
Incognito pen-pal lovers lurk behind their scripts
exchanging words a poor excuse for real fucking
        obviates the banquet sense
    for souls are ruled by eyes
gazing at the cast of aluminum Baltic sky
   without the gaze to meat
young minds take off with endless sway.

But Artists,
Make to give pleasure.
Courtesans in poetic whoredom
juggle fire on the tongue's
                tongs.

Like summer's final thunderstorm
Flashes, spiraling, unwinding
Opening traces of nitrogen , ozone, growth excitatory
Priapic
        choice
Minions gather for a symposium of sight.

Guardians of Watchtowers
the elemental king's released
    clockwise, winds
        whose time-sight
Linea Filii Sancti
we go out under our eyes   Spread, Spread out and see
                                   In fluid triumph children we

Demon's counter wisdom
unwinds truly
as does offering ecstasy orally
    & take this as you may
or delivering deep massage with knowing hands
                form back-words
messages maintain
    true counter clock-wise ways
        Wisdom's kingdom
     Nerves listen with feeling
  to the rising spirit.
  Youth fool(s).
     Taking turns together
We   give
     It up.

                       Dedicated to the gentle soul
                   and subtle wit of Deryk Burton
                      who passed on 10/ 9/ 97

A Course of Charges & Apparitions

For Barb

ozazam urelp,

(tr. make me a strong seething)

2nd Enochian Call

I've heard the Djinn
will strip you down,
not gin, but genie
a root to ingenuity
lord of spirit of fire,
salamanders,
down to essentials
can take the form of all
the lovers that ever
cut to the quick,
lettered their writhing bodies
spell
A secret code of positions
a psycho-sexed brand
in the memory hide
to evoke a feeling emulsion
names itself
lamen, emotion, a spike in the eye.

II   Bark as Facade
I have seen myself
where lightning has blasted
cambium from the apex of a tree
the Japanese call Jin this sacred surface
protection removed and still healthy.

And I've listened to sister
thunder an index, pure
void of cogitation
as a majestic atemporal utterance
its speed eliminates the question
why with consumptive wonder.
Pitch, key, and tempo collide full spectrum
black and all-inclusive.

III   Pentecostal Holocaust
Crown burning
to speak in tongues
the tastebuds & pink soft cells
are a rendering   plant
making scoria and carnage
into a primal slur(y
glue that holds life's images
in a chain—vignette, or collage

for divination a poet's job
is random shuffling
to embrace chance / instants.

The lifetime movement and happening
        is the vision uncloaked
        into the oracular by silence
            sings the mind.
There is no disruption near cicada's din
Heat is pure / Hekt,
                                sweat's hydromel.
The image dripping off your brow
        Should not be lost
this unction rubbed into a lover's
        glands speaks to their touch
        a host beat gold leaf thin
        and spread the surface of a soul
        will carry life on to the next
        strand in our gauze of great being
the see-through veils you never saw.

7/27/99

A Comforting Terror
                    (for Chuck Stein)

Does not come from the feeling
arises from somewhere between
soft cushioned theater seats
and the vampire on the screen.

A stricken etymology of the Tau + error
                        the delphic E starts off the rumble
mind full of matter's pull.

Presents
not a life-threat but
a presence pretty
buttons & stems of destroying angels
so soft, milk white, and deadly
pleasing to the eye
                        tongue—acrid sting.

Or a cute voodoo doll
to take home for a night but
instead it's just to descry
those wonderful curves,
death dealing lines
where pins take no cushion
if it were a victim in its stead
I cannot repeat the points that bled
true roseate display of wonder

in animus, simulacra stuffing,
for real guts

from dreams.

A world of wake-believe
shunted desires through a sleep
bound by a crash
where no rest is found
for demons hurl spears & winnowing darts
at trains carrying real aspirations
that cannot stop
                or let on
something not
                ever getting off
without the necessary attention
dearly paid for
        or totally cast away
hold tightly, let go lightly and be saved.

Love is a golden bubble full of dreams
that waking breaks, and fills us with extremes.
by wild means
there is no safety in our encounters
boundaries, simple, that we cannot
cross but in a solvent fluid field.

Where stranger love happens
to your world shakes
                    beams shoot in then re-align
                        some will to a way
                                upset to set up new
for the crucial play
that can raise mud up to passion stars
    like nothing else
drifting silt in the celestial sea
we'll never settle.

Insistence

Liquid light pours
sun shot dew
from leaves, *sutras*,
drops
that anoint the brow or face
are the most sacred.

A cowl of haze
embraced by my neck
your humid breath's spread
& eyes,
seeds of sanguine sleep
in the batrachian night
noise
swallowing thoughts
impressions in the hollow
core's persistence
to compress sound
like sea shells
issue the ocean
far from water.

Is the unspoken fundamental
truth   contained   space
nestled in the small of the back
arched upon a firm surface

the crown feeds
from constellations,
excrement,
the spring peepers
hiding low in the ravine
sing.

Thel(e)ma and Louise

Do you bless
flies and ants
before swatting
and sending them to the light

Θελημα
the lamia
a Christabel perhaps
swooned by a poet
in opiate *res*
a real beast sucker
that lurks steadily
closer with each sleep.

You & some unholy numbered few
humanize negative integers.

III

Berthing Beyond

Surrounding vision of a stone ring
gray rugose granite
the size of ancient money
tilted at an angle so its hole can make a seat.

A dome asylum of infinite axes
born in the blessed morning reverie
as from suffumigating O's
                    soporific perfume
                            laid-in-sense,

We will make our home with
a hold up on the cold slab
                    foundation
sod peeled up roof maid of sky
from Yesod to throat for song
layered spirits in the wind
answered why the need to anchor in some lair
                    was left unheeded movements only
Know the key is hard to find
when the trance begins to lift.

II

This,   demonstrative act
Awakening with my dreams hypnotic
words wholly suffer no more mutes
& stops for naught,

Absorbing the process is all that seams matter,
                                        I mean all that seems to matter.

III

          Perspectiva
    That great art of arts
    Alberti is to be thanked for
    at the Gallery's opening

Pyramid of vision, more of a cone,
                                        a gyre in itself
                          & the fire of the eye
                          pyrating all it sees
    Inverted, a will to covet
again metabolize and reduce the field of vision
to a mere repast for thought
Bobs about on the terr-
aqueous sea of the eye.

When the last lid lowers on
all this shored up
Wisdom will nestle around the elliptic
          gate of the ancients
Awaiting the circle's break
for some movement beyond
the cave.

Possession

Because ownership is in the hands of the Gods
eye made, home grown,

                      evocation of emotions.
      The sycamore tree that spreads the old
      man's essence from his roots
      up from the trunk by the corner of Farm Brook and Wood Bridge
      , streets that call up country,
& the creek just at the right level, its flow
gurgle pitched to consume attention
        then sooth
as it's all about
forgetting the past
           up till   caught-by-the-moment(um)
                as deity reflects
             enough of not being God
                              spheres of love
                            meet, react to that reaction.

Plenitude
   if any more can dance through me
     I should burst at the seams.

           Eyes studying, wider and wider till the woods
                  alive with spiraling
                  fields become visible
                   energy grows and rises from
                  the composting killed floor.

The Living Lament

In memoriam Eleanor Podgurski née Fiedler

1/9/1921 to 10/30/2005

An air coming from another world,
sad, plaintive, ever-inviting a few
creatures enlist for their own self-same finale'.

Others sing caught-me-naught
surrounded before death by the drones
       hypnotizing
through the most powerful harmonies
  and muscle building emotions come in
strains with the ultimate past arousal.

But do the dead lament the living as we know them
    (the living demented)
We who have begun motioning toward a light of reflection.
Not all in sight
     grown or nurtured from states of being,
   not-being created out of confusion
   unknowing in such cases
     intuit in aeternitas
       immediate
       and waking every second
Revere the release and revel
     perpetually in surrendering to death always at hand

projecting infinity from that womb
Sudden death brings sudden life
          to a select coterie

          —Shaivite—

eyes open to meet the object
after all a stone becomes a star in matters of the heart
insignia of a furiously led life.

—Rites of Passage—

<u>Extreme</u> Unction so modern,
,sounding,
but Catholics no longer get
the oil on their dead
maybe because it is all too extreme
          for spiritual light-weights
          do not move into the light on a daily basis
          and would not know how the dead could
          ever bless them in turn.
     The animadversion's won
contemplating certification of the dead
recognize the irreal officially
after all identity is up for grabs.

—**Mourning Process**—

Actual waste of the body
and mind in body mirror each other
      if taken by the light
      something speaks to me
      through these coded parallel paths
      an angel and a loa cooperate
      to mark a revealing trait.
                    —Take notice
The angel's share
      offered up as breath and song
      escapes containment of such clutching
      vessels before the thirsty mouth arrives and rests upon the rim.

Her final breath's wisdom
sent in
      between sleep and awareness
I was bathed in thick binding light flashes
clearing the visual path in that self-same room
where I first slept as a child and often woke
in fear that I had passed eternities and traveled far
               so lucky to make it back.

Indeed, a Spell to bring the living to the fold
  again
 noble in every vibration & distinction
      Moving away from the decomposed
      to allow the nigredo to consume the dross & inert.

—Unbirthing—

Renewing those old child eyes on the illuminated
carpet of golden fall leaves at my feet
required following their radiance due
wind, rain and fiery hue in extension of reactions outpouring.
When I see the light I see so little
primitive reality balanced on the edge
conscious only with time does it settle
& sear through glands straight to my pineal
to know I must taste when I have consumed
the orphaned double.
Here's a cannibalizing root wonder
with no regrets
and there is little more one can ask for.

Muscle Memory

(To Horace Bush)

Into submission or it will run a practical course
'en route to the quotidian register of dreadful banality.

Reminiscences of the distant past
        varying legacies
                inherited in limbs.

My Slavic blood
immersed with the Mongol has left
                a right arm of ancestral aggression
High on the strike, prevalent
making it hard to harness while telegraphing
revolts   are good
                Life forces ways into
mind's
every striation,
a conflict encountered, the overthrow
pivots on a minor regime mute
shouldered,
                talking in twitches
tendon
        quivers,
the taut line
        made a bow
for taking low shots on characters.

Parts of a weapon anatomical
chapter of skirmish and battle
stored for reckoning
volatile bursts of anger,

        restraints of parts
populate the warring body
        politic,
                and if they offend
                        start sharpening the axe
                                        (a quill.

Emerging through the gene pool
Dominant
                kicking the recessive's ass
dropping some nucleic acid into obscurity
that mentality bred within the collective body
and the flesh ticks, twitches are the signs that fight
is brewing against
                gentle thoughts
                are unsuccessful
                in these stages
wherefore the soothing stroke mistaken for an assault
        goes, not postal, but into letters
        drawn out of chaos
deeply kneading nerves
                and gently shifting soul
into liberation's way to read
                        motion on contact.

Squaring of the Fleshy Circle

The Gods told man to bend over
giving us:
         Prometheus on a stick.
Flavored to meet our tongues' flaming
Needs
        Fanning
        Immolation
        His banquet
      Off(ering
                No extinguisher,
           No law,
      No escape,
          Quarter.

Grendlevania

Adults Store
Limbs
We take them
Seriously here
Licensed to quarter / lose some.

The large dark man in the Restaurant
discussed an extended penis plan
over his fried green Mitchell.

While the christian couple
said Race
            at the neighboring table.
Old time religion,   Fungal,   For you and me.

In The Shadow of Big Ben

Plain understanding of pattern overlay
          dew upon an orb-weaver's mesh
          magnifier of the micro
          intersects that stage
others should be sufficient
        only that some spider's discarded prey, a dried ant
        made its way next to John's Yorkshire pudding.
              The desire to secrete
            certain substances
        does not overwhelm
                  in doppler waves pushed out
                    from the moment
               radiating in an expanding circumference.

Say the spirit spinning is spider-like
        under the food of your breath
           generate some wisdom
        of the sort our black and white cat
          knows to hunt by.

A wheel swirl
circularity power link
in motion,
      without the weave
    is inert.

Language dreaming
upon ourselves empirical
                       & cerebral
the code entanglement
rapid eyes move over it
                         however the slower ones digest

As I was told
"until you eat with your eyes
open you
are not a hunter"
providers never leave us
living on infinite planes.

Artists decompose in their graves,
so after they've died
their works go backwards
till they disappear was the jest,
the Mozart joke in a graveyard
punch-
         line
                proving that you
have to take it with you
back to the source, in a sense
after common thought would dispose of the art
        Lost to a cell,
          memory,

A mariner imperceptible to the sense
brought us in and out
spiriting in the quest
for consciousness altering utterances
taken to heart.

Having been at the ocean
          and headed in-
                    land
          I am at a loss for sea vision
          locked into the sun, sand, and salt
          covered flesh is so tranquilized.

Sunsets power into the crystals of a crag
     embeds the glow
               between
day and night, orange and red
the power of silence is so different in twilight
skrying with ease
                    on a gate left open.
The pure force that surrounds in
          sentinels,
an ally's cargo
                    navigated through open
musings, lost
          to surf on air-waves of dreamers
          and be metabolized in due course.

                    From the urban piedmont to Sullivan's Point
                         to Dixon's Ridge at end.

Killing Reason

> "Life is more akin to a jungle…
> if it's fulfillment you seek,
> best bring a machete."
> from Michelle Croft's Blog

On October 11, 07, Michelle Croft pulled out a shotgun
shot her son, Daath, to death as he slept, never to waken
and then herself in an apartment
Just off of New Hope Road in Gastonia, North Carolina.

She was divorced and Daath's natural father, Torch Locklear was devastated
and so was Daath's brother, Forest, 16, living in Florida
Daath / Torch / Forest
                        Formula of a southern headless purging ritual
taking away the parent in the child.

The abyss of reason, swallowing useless words
erasing clarified intent, what else can a family know
so all that's left is blood
relations offending sensibilities, morals, and needs
the basics of interaction too often put on hold
then the hurt grows uncontrollably
till it's done
                all about everything close by.
The chemistry of Choronzon
an abysmal body functioning off the dross personality decocted
out of a vacuum, his nature, contra naturam
abhors nothing, where naught is home—the family is taken to the morgue.

Cabalistically divorced
head from body from kin
contends with qliphoth creeping into
the light of the leaves, falling.
What these shells do when ignored
is breaking
          all hell
             loosened
the distance of the fall is fantastic from any perspective.

Impregnated mind, fleshy brain
          The 5th Aethyr, LIT admonished Perdurabo:
"thou art so dull of understanding…for all thou thinkest
is but thy thought" the mind's the devil's workshop
forging away on the innocent reason, young playful soul.

Undertaking the judgment call
landing into a relationship
pulled downward
in order to plant and gestate
rather than bury
voices drowned out by blood
nourished topsoil covers the grave entirely.

Thereafter, a little ways down the road
from the scene of the crime
on South New Hope
a grove was bulldozed for a new
Food Lion.

And for a time a single large oak was left standing
eventually hacked down like the rest
according to the barren   rules.

Collapsing in the silenced
offspring sacrificed long before the death
by a beast that roams and kills
at will in a cage of alternating light
and form / stripes, the bars
to disappear in the darkness
perversely turned on.

                                        12/9/2007

Grasp

How addicted we are to seizures
all encapsulated in the clutch
poor desirous hatchlings
looking to grasp
        satiety
        & in turn possession takes
ambient psychology applied
whether or not the system can handle it.

Uroborous barnacle,
sensation
the latest
what a fad
takes everything for a ride
pan-psychistic conquests
for the allure
everything is overwhelming
and leads to nothing.

A hold of this is worth far more
than ever,
      never,
        savor,
again

    How seized we are by addiction to Death.

        Italicized quotes from Hugo Ball's
          expressionist assault

(Untitled)

The movable letters on the sign
spelled out:
      "All fried down to earth"
some ancient form of south'rn alchemy
boiled in grease the hide is
turned to plating,
   flesh and soft muscles
reduced to a hardened *nigredo*
no longer of use for the skeleton remains.

Rebel Departure

The Intentionally lost
cause of the Thelemic Confederacy
Operation Southern Star
has begun to dismantle
the disunion and secede from fascism and state.

The need for inducting Shaivite priests is great
and to chronicle the cabinet of tantric fiasco
control with Bardic wailings.

The native and beast will come out from their caves
Our officers must stand back and listen carefully
to their cries, summons to fire
only when they see the darkness of lies.

Phase II

Behead the state
Usher in the bornless
 rule under will-
less law
Down so far
south to signal
an essential independence
signaling
deep ones to spread

order of disorder
where the few who can see
will list(en) up
against the hole
summons Soul-full food.

Phase I

The house is as not,
a hold, a keep,
compound of the ill-at-ease
polity in duress
except in the minds of the rebel
swells, hell eon, the fruition of the Kali yuga
the black-house is right here, not over yonder,
with the loyal sons of the angst orbited
faith,
       Watchers,
            maintaining the threshold,
                line
              bisecting the light and dark worlds
              the stars broadcast
              and the stripes, a reminder of pain
              that is not always a liberator…

Naught structures
Swamps reclaim these old estates
     in decrepitude
     the systemic

                lumbering
                goings on
        where there lurks the green
                Goddess
                    algae draped
                            kelp crowned
                                and her bed of wormwood,
                                wermut, belies her undergrowth
                                studying the swimming potential
                                            spermatozoon
                                flow'n
                                'round.

Insurrection of the land
mirrored in the revolting
souls buried
beneath the party-line
drawn,
            beneath pitched conflicts
            throw away troops
mulched
            over
                    that must be forgotten
                        in order to fulfill their purpose.

Summoned to the cause by shrieks
Goetic rebel howls
housing Gehenna
made of the wood of un-
fulfilled desires fed by the blood

letting confederate priest-hood,
the old southern giants—live oaks—rise up
out of the terrible ground
fed on the water-of-life
and nameless
                        still
witness to the trouble that never left
ignored, erupts into other wars.

Phase O

                The battle for the hill to stand upon
                and increase the field of visual rays fanning out
                fertile and profound
        as ventured by the lonely farmer
descrying the crop's growth
under the last rays of sun-
set devil worship
                aggression of all directions
                without a single slave to pull,
                plow the coveted can run
                feral growths across the border
                and without a boundary we have
                space to share,
                the air provides an infinite room
                housing breath with bodies
                on the intake.

Each image recalled on the mount:
beasts of the home-front are field-foraging
to bring more sustenance, fruit
bearing the lower body
cleansed, stripped of thread worn
flesh of the whip discarded
so the gentle physique left alone
will carry liberation to the ground,
that theater of revealing
winning with each runaway inspiration's train,
liberation emerges from below

        same as a bunch of green peanuts
        about to be boiled speak of the main course
        their colors change under the careful watch,
        heat, and salt…

      Down (ward focused

cross-hairs become sights,   grave markers

      optic grid coordinates

do little to reveal the rarest honey
made by the dying bees
paradise lost to the victors
indiscernible,
discredited,
graceless.

Mountain Sent

The moment
that is full of the earth

is full

Ken Irby

from *Variations: 13*

A perfect fire ignites
out of ecstatic providence   from the top down
upon carefully layered kindling,

           logs,

for survival   set   needs   branches of the self-
same passion
    enables the able
        supple limbs upon the trunk
    from the crown down   pathway blazing
    the same applies to our bodies caught in this illuminating descent
    unveiled in the coupling opposites   the third arises
union   reaction
flames spreading downwards
        dictated by the eye of the spark.

So much light
    reflected off the fresh fallen snow
    rare now, even up higher in the Blueridge Mountains
    the storm of 16th, February 13
        caught everyone off-guard

On the other side
        at the courthouse falls
a peculiar absence
        of snow   nonetheless had the stream running high.
        At camp the fire immolates inward
bestowed   3 lone logs   fan outward flames
a devil's pitchfork,
                The center tine   hollowed out   a hummingbird's silhouette
fashioned so delicately, long and slender, a sickle bill
        now pulsing out of the orange scarlet heart of ember glow
        ebbing and waxing   this self-tending   furnace
going for hours   untouched   how the solitary survive   by maintaining
their grip,
                and hedge bets
                        by banking their coals   accordingly   the beloved
                                has wings
                        given
                                to volatile displays
                                                caprice
                                                and departure
                        upon trains   of indecipherable thought.

At any given point on the ridge-line
                the snowfall rate varied
The parkway bare on the border of Shining Rock
but back on the Art Loeb and Mountains-to-Sea Trail
                                it was deepening
        No view   from the Devil's Courthouse.

White – Out conditions prevailed
the cloud ceiling so low   as if the sky's bottom fell out
above   and below   coalescing in the dissolution of vision's   field.

All those giant Mountain Laurel and Rhododendron's
        thousands of buds, dormant
violet hues encased   hidden passions under
                protection of the snow's   wall of winter warmth.

How long to hold out   for the opening

& return from the woods   with skills born   bush-wise
                and honed axe edge   ground sense
        freshly split humour and nerve
                balls out
                        bearing   on
                                        magnetic north
                Ultima Thule   destiny   coordinates
        along certain lines / life
that fire building sensibility creeps down
its kinetic traveling cell to cell from cognition to ignition
spread by the metabolic inferno
carrying swatches of wonderment
in a survival sack   for all ways   take notice
never running, but living outside   of time.

In Memoriam
Stevie the Cat
A more loyal companion
There will never be
6/13/2013

102

Shift in perspective came about while giving Williams dictum "No ideas but in Things" its due consideration, and some Sherman Paul essays. My path as it has dictated / directed my workings as of late prompted me to carry William's notion to its logical, or rather, magical conclusion or antithetical progression: No perceptions but in the *back of beyond*[1] things (being a root center). This tendency to gravitate towards naught is obviously problematic as in certain circumstances employing verbal discourse to elaborate on such skryings is to run counter to or more accurately under-cut the actual experience. If it is truly the shadow then to attempt to merge it with the tonal or daylit realm then it becomes potentially dissolute. Respect the space seems to be the dictum if there is one.

This is where Gertrude Stein's sentiment that the poet cannot be afraid to wander comes across as a key admonition. The creative meandering or "Wandering on Course" as I have termed it in the past is the motion and

---

1   This phrase I adopted from chapter II of Horace Kephart's *Our Southern Highlanders*

kinetic for entering the field. As Blaser stated, You've
"got to not know what the hell you're doing" to make
this approach work. To wander focused in the Scotian
Cloud of Unknowing as it were is a defining progression.
Consciously directing the process will short-circuit it.
The un-direction of the field rides me as it were. A Sufi /
Ducanesque approach.

1/10/2013

As I wrap up my first collection of poems in my
project(ive Wandering on Course it finally came to me
and not consciously directed is a new project, (En)
Closure of the Unexplored. It popped up organically out
of winding up Wandering and it clearly is an antithesis to
the opening of the field. I'd have to say I see it as not that
the field is closing but the wilderness, the collapsed and
decayed ground being reclaimed by the wild. Chernobyl,
perfect example of this. And this wilderness is analogous
to the inner self alienated by the fixation with the
cyber mechanoid media blitz, Ipads, phones, internet
all distracting self from inner-self, ie the abandoned
wilderness / energy field (Duncan also looked at Field
poetics as energy or electro-magnetic protoplasmic
field of energy. Oh well, thought you may find my new
embarkation a point of interest.

1/21/2013 (email to Peteris and Agnes)

Oops.   Left out one revision. It took a while but
I finally got it succinct.   Instead of the En Closure of
the unexplored, it should read: Exposure from the
Unexplored.   This really nails it on the head because the
unexplored or the inexplicable can remain so even in its
exposure but in being disclosed even at a distance it has an
effect upon the observer / reader just like we can see 4 stars
being born in Orion's Nebula, can't really explore it but it
presents its own exposure sending out its image and like
an old fashioned film negative it leaves its likeness etched
upon the retina.

1/19/2013

Olson saw the field as real, fecund, tangible to be walked
into, impregnated, embraced, explored. Duncan saw the
field as something invoked and allowed to possess the
self thereby. To me the field is or rather what is at stake
in re the field is the root nascent energy of the organic.
The micoriza, the strange bacteria and mold that make
the soil able to germinate and hold the plants, trees, life.
And so it is the backside of it all, the unutterable and the
inconceivable that backs up the drive or inspiriting agent
of the utterance that fascinates and compels me. This

project though is as Sir Thomas Browne stated: "Thy will
be done though in my own undoing" or the daunting
task of attempting to articulate this underpinning
relationship at hand that refuses to speak in intelligible
terms.

1/23/2013

Even more strange is that the phrase, Exposure From the
Unexplored is a projection of itself. I can only partially
come to terms with what it implies but I am not able
to understand it. It leads but does not plot a course to
any terminus.   Rather it is in one sense an extension
of Mallarme's *Un Coup De Des*.   The dice throws or
rather controls the hand that casts it. Reverse motion in
motion at its inception. This poetics posits a meditation
on the ain soph, the Kabbalistic limitless light beyond
the veils of negative existence. It is pure antithesis and
is problematic from a poetic standpoint. As Heidegger
stated something to the effect that it is as futile to write
about nothing as it is to speak about silence. Well, yes
and no. There is a sense, a feeling here to be conveyed.
And this Exposure is as much a branch of magick and
meditation as much as a poetics. Whether or not it
manifests as written verse is inconsequential.

The Concealing Voice

Ever since Delphi
          we knew they were hiding something
          the oracles, the words
                         as if by commandment
                                      split meaning
               & headed for the hills.
          Craniums alight took off
                         swaths of interpretation
                         seemingly to get it.

That was all gas
                         or was it just
                         out of the earth seepings
          Beat our heads against rocks
                         why don't we
                         for the stars will come out
                              in this Pan'd night
                              that keeps the unreadable
                              but very real energizing script
                                      under wraps.

Her warm moist breath
               spread out upon my senses
          through lips poised to kiss
               the message.
          Enrolled in a bliss rapt in-tension
               (more than can be said
          to light a lamp in the aether
               of my mind's ear.

On this leg   listening   is right here
            they say "it's hard to say."
            Firm is the denial haunting
            inspiration's thrust.
      P. tells me, "not good—howling all night"
      the goetia's meddling
             the harsh Goddess peddling
            wares of lust
         come out in a moment   arresting

Crow's echo people's echo
            her, high up in the hickories & red oaks
            repeating caws beckon gut responses.
            Across the sea D. tells me
            they call
            river ice flows: *Okrao*
            as it breaks up sounding of cordivae
            a multiplex murder (of) shows
                  air at once.
The will can be killed
                  she says
      however displaying
a great difference between feeling
                  and being weak.

III

    —Phase Shifts—

                    Angel's share
                    the demon's take
                    an illicit thirst
                    of dark souls slaked
                    before they counter
                    round the bend
                    and mirrored leap
                    each other's end...

From little miss-information's
        fickle governance
where even the slightest illness
        alters the vision
strange static & absurd images
populate the visionary's field.
This lack of continuity though
        clarifies in its own plane
coherence may speak to me
        of her plan
            & puzzle-
    ment
        altered motion.

IV
What has been breathed in
        from the past
            (bin)
        never emptied
            tenacious residue adheres
        the lungs integuments
                fashion being
        beads of moisture sensation
                in condensation.
     Light seeds the precipitating
     speech
back(ing of words
        back of brain stem(ming
from primal images inducing immediacy's utterance
a simple stop,   _uh_
        visceral /glottal
        phonemically strangled
                off the top of meaning's
        scale from n(one to multiply
                beyond.

V

Muted
        Tawny brown russet
                death leaves
    in winter
        on eastern deciduous forest floors

meaning
        muted death   leaves

Stripped down scenes
dried green fruticose lichen
    neon
            distracts
                from all the solid
granite grown over
                its variegated
                mineral design
                eaten into by the organic
                growth, engraving symbiotic
                        relationship for millennia.

VI
Apocrypha and the unverifiable.
What is it we must always have
in seeking authority   out
                a life invested in a writ?
        Fragments especially
                from the Dead Sea,
                        or Parmenides,
                        Nag Hammadi.
                                et cetera.

The crumbled away
                intentions along
with the disintegrated parchment
somehow are filled in
        by desire
        a yearning for completeness
—the specter
        of these departed texts
                        overshadows
                        under shadows.

VII

Leaving the trail be-
      hind
     be hare,
           be raven
   with innate, instinctual movement
        guided headings.
Being really lost brings discovery,
    Walking   methodically,
      because speed limits
                awareness
                     of details
                          growing.

                              Robert Podgurski
                              12/17/12 – 1/6/2013

Here is where this work begins
a conversation with Bob Podgurski

SD: …getting the antenna up, strikes me, as in the double-wand of the oracularization of the work, to be the work's inmost self as it comes out or IS out. …much more to talk about but I like in your double-wanded yes a great little manifest and call to urge out the writing...

RP: I am thinking of Duncan's issue about being obedient to the poem. This sucked me back into my understanding of the Australian aborigines dreamtime, continual never-ending coming into being creation imagining its own inception, etc., etc.. Then the "Dreams interpreted without your will" what we all do in doing violence to the world and nature at large. And what ultimately is at stake here in this poem is the amorphous realm, the deep, its impenetrable nature and defiance of description.

It's funny, I have had a batch of Chthonic, Lovecraftian influenced poems that were supposed to be published at one point and the press that was going to do it went under. In fact, that's happened a couple of times. My cursed poesy. (You've already seen a sample of it in "Jimson's Gift" "Spiderplant," "Oyster Gem," etc.) For me the glimpses of this realm have been far more fleeting hence the brevity of the pieces. I catch certain glimpses in flashes and keep these theophanies short so as not to wreck the moment. Whether or not I'm doing it any justice remains to be seen. But since I've done chthonic magic I'm more interested in allowing my consciousness to be pulled down / apart / and travel into the deep qliphothic tunnels, learn un-control, etc.

SD: I think what keeps the entirety of poetic production, en masse, not just us or one to one but the all of it, completely rat poison, is the sense of writing for the end. So the end gets to become viral. But we all know that what's happening with the media, the big media, the feeding frenzy too, but it is personal—is just our standard of living.

Psyche-logos would attempt a way into that seance, that levitation, in order to get at the drives behind these figures and symbols. It would be done best in a trance. Yes, how are we organized? If we are trapped inside of our own language, and it's what we made, then we should be able to unmake it? Maybe if we stop trying to be so grammatically logical, that's the key. Your use of the qliphothic, the metaphoric shell as underground, is at work thru your attention to the poem thru-out its being composed. Is this a new age?

RP: I swear I've engaged in *Double Wanded* because as Roger Gilbert Lecomte wrote in his one poem, I want to be confused, but in the sense of what Robin Blaser said about the serial poem, that a poet has got to *not* know what the hell he's doing. And I think that's important insofar as not striving to control and/or direct the poem but allowing it to dictate and lead the poet. That's why I've always had such a hard time writing fiction although I'm getting a little better at it. As soon as I have an idea of the ending it loses all of its momentum for me. So I've learned all these games of how to let myself get distracted by minutiae of the piece and let it take me to a space I had never considered and effect the final outcome, etc. At some point I'll forward some of my short stories to you, one or two are ok.

SD: Because obviously no one has read _______ there in this new context, or anyone else for that matter, just the narrow context they were putting them thru, like a rock star, yesterday. Silliness.

And yes re Jonathan Williams. I start my memory book thingey just re-writing again with plunge into *Book of the Green Man* and remind it was a hiking book begun in Appalachia, but he is in it, to sense nearness is the point.

Far out, rob!

RP: Well, the *Red Book* is such an interesting piece in this puzzle. An amazing redaction of Jung's inner committee held sway under the Christo-centric central scrutinizer. However, it is a brilliant risk taken in the game as we've come to know it. He took the chance, bared some really tough corners of his closet-soul but confined it to the writing. Acting it out would have been anathema to the old boy and if he did it would have had to wind up with a not-so-healthy self-crucifixion not to undercut the importance of the work. Jung was the first to scientifically approach the dark recesses whereas Freud was all gut-level assessment thereof. I firmly believe Jung took it about as far he possibly could have given his overall project.

But insofar as misunderstanding Wittgenstein is concerned the same goes for Derrida. I mean, to get into Derrida please people take the time to read most of Rousseau, Plato, and Aristotle and get back to me in a few years. Wittgenstein's erudition, and the underpinnings thereof factored into his opaque ratiocinations are even more of a conundrum to dig through . But hey, if we placed any substantial queries to lit critters and took them to task on folks fiddling with these matters a lot of people would be out of jobs, department chairs vacated, and grad students heading downstream without any paddle or place to publish their specious horseshit. Man, it would be a nicer world wouldn't it. I really don't need to get started on any of this.

Well my stories are just story-telling or at least an attempt to be, to foster a tail spinning voice like I've heard in the Appalachians here. Jonathan Williams was pretty smart to pay attention to all of what was near him. I can appreciate that aspect of being here deep in the red. Like I said, at some point I'll get you a few, just don't count on anything too intricate or profoundly literate.

SD: So great with the synchronic here, noting it, and it is duly noted how the difference between the drives of academia and the drives of our larger, more bludgeoning culture in the real world run between a poly-chromatic dreamweaver and analytical sobriety both, as I see it, so that working in words as descriptors in a university setting is tantamount to the naivete of child's play, whereas words and images of commerciality and commodification seem to ray out in incredibly rich and diverse quasi realizations, their manifold realizations of theft and also of conjuring. But we are living in the illusion that we can separate these two realities, the academic from the commercial, and come up with some notion of fair play and also some real *Homo Ludens*. We come up with nothing and we end up exactly where this whole thing began: a very wild and perverse orgy of interests still vying for control over a 'new world.' One thing's for certain: we have to stay safe as everything goes to hell. Self-preservation seems to be the embodiment of the new.

RP: As far as I'm concerned if you want to get the most out of Duncan take the time to read him under the neoplatonic / magical / Freudian / etc., Jaussian approach. I just mention Hans Robert Jauss off the cuff because his thing where you can take at any given point in someone's oeuvre a synchronic bisection of influences along a diachronic line of work is illustrative of the vast realm that has to be considered.

And it's that synchronic field of multiplex and pertinent factors that's got to govern the critical course charted if someone's hoping to get at the real deal. However, this isn't a good readymade formula for folks on the tenure track, etc. It's just too old fashioned and labor intensive, and in the case of modern criticism, sort of counter-productive in that it tends to make one want to keep one's mouth shut until the jury's back in that's typically out for an extremely long deliberation.

SD: Bravo, rob. Damn straight! That's exactly where the infantilism has its start, in the vacuum of maya. I remember picking up that crap book about the end of history by what's his face and the problem is these children have no idea about time and space even. Expand the mind when you can, don't put it off for later. But education has to be an industry, otherwise we won't be free. That's why we just throw books at them. We think if we hit them in the head *and* the pocket-book with books they'll sink into the kids' skulls deeper. And that has a ripple effect out to other endeavors too, even those with great intention and intensity, so that the projections overwhelm every point of view.

RP: Well, I'm not so naive as to assert some of purity of aims and or methodologies of the artist vs. the academic. Rather my concern is that within let's say the typical English dept. where the average grad student is required to take a critical theory 101, etc., and in that indoctrination over 90 days or so be exposed to a smattering of deconstruction, reader-response, Northrop Frye, Harold Bloom, etc., etc., and that this more or less marks the start of the making of a critic. And furthermore, that criticism is somehow to be distinguished from creative writing.

I always have to laugh: I had a cousin who ran a law department and knew that I wrote poetry and asked me if I was going to study creative writing in Grad school. I merely rejoindered with no, I'm in literature and am thus working on non-creative writing as it were. But I digress. More to the point I see a tradition of the <u>non</u>-academic scholar, Coleridge for example, as a key counter-agent. STC was in no way affiliated with the academy and he almost single-handedly opened up the cauldron of critical enquiry a la Kant, Fichte, Schelling, etc. In his own fashion he helped to pave the way for modern philological studies (now out of fashion in Amerika I might add) amongst other areas of study in criticism. This type of independent scholar is often responsible for refreshing and revitalizing an otherwise stagnant morass. Ken Warren's one of the few out there who comes along to successfully work this vein. *Captain Poetry's Sucker Punch* has got some great fucking shit in it doesn't it?

As I always used to joke with my mentor at CU Boulder, John Murphy, the hermeneutic process has gone into an interminable spin dry cycle and the lint catcher just ain't work'n any more. This is your mind on fuzz, I would say, and he'd get a big kick out of it. But sadly it is true. Unless the average grad student has a somewhat enlightened old-timer to help guide them along then they just plod along in the vacuum of maya taking the ubiquitous illusion for the real thing. And that is also where folks become mired in this bizarre hegemonic vying of one approach or school over another for some position of primacy in the thrust to get it right. As we probably agree it's difficult to get something right when one doesn't even know what the hell the questions are. Therefore I agree with you whole-heartedy we have to stay safe by risking it all in crossing the abyss of reason (and I do mean making it across as well as vexing the damn monster). Williams was right, men die every day for lack of what is found here.

Was hesitating on my final last missive as the discussion was getting
a bit drawn out but glad I did. For one thing, this last reply helped to
elucidate your expanded sense of 'industry.' I mean, it wasn't that it
was unclear to me but the entire realm encompassed, cross-referenced,
and its unfortunate fall-out you've implied is now in my crosshairs.
The commodification of lit crit is problematic only insofar as it's
appropriated, nay, hamstrung as a job-retaining measure for academics.
The payoff is grim for the factory as well as the end user. And the
infantilism (I like that, I'm going to go back to that term instead of the
ever popular 'dumbed down') represents a real morass.

Btw, I checked out the Ambix collection elsewhere just to make sure,
and Weiser's does have the deal. The best from amazon marketplace
was $56 used.   I think you'll be well served by that collection of essays
for an unbeatable price. Has some of Lynn Thorndike's old essays in it
I've been meaning to read. I have referenced his *A History of Magic and
Experimental Science*, 8 volumes from time to time. Are you familiar
with it? It's dated but pretty comprehensive much like Frazier's
Golden Bough full expanded version, a solid old bulwark in its own
right.

SD: The entire dream of culture as well as the physiognomy of dream
is what is embedded in the image. It's the mercurial, no? We can
debate these things but in *3 sea monsters* I just wanted to have the
background as historical become literal séance so that the 'reasons'
for the shape of poems and literature wouldn't be seen as causes. If it
is more organic, the organization and reception, then it doesn't have
to live up to the non-existent standards of a scene, which is basically
kids who have been shown a picture of what they are supposed to
be thinking and feeling in regards to the production of poems and
pictures.

We just watched a documentary on Gerhardt Richter and I came away
impressed. I thought I wouldn't like it or him but I did. He is physically
moving the paint not so much onto the canvas but ONTO THE PICTURE,
THE RECEIVED CULTURAL IMPOSITION OF PICTURE and he is doing
it with his entire body sometimes. So his making is free and NOT chained
to the conceptual as chained to the production line of meaning which
would only be there to justify the prevailing view of matter and energy,
all those causes and effects, but he is there to work with the art, what is
being received. At one point, in a gallery filled with Picassos for a show at
a museum, he is looking up at the skylight and musing on the scaffolds in
the museum's ceilings and his eyes not even once come into contact with
the Picassos, many of which were *incredibly* interesting.

E=MCsquared is also an economic concept because it became influential.
All the influences don't necessarily come forth in a linear, preconceived
way, of course. When American poetry finally realized it could be a simple
brush stroke, and as Snyder early on indicated too he wanted to go to
China not Japan but it was closed, that was a very important moment
(whether it's recognized as important or not). Snyder is almost exclusively
a preacher in some twisted way later, or it's more pronounced later, but
the point is to encounter this is also in the séance with Fenollosa and his
embodiment of the wabi-sabi type view, or trying to grasp it, the thing on
poetry that Pound took is only one part of the view he wanted to present.
And Yeats, like you say, is fucking powerful, beyond the other aspects
of his personality, yes, I think those plays are really interesting too, he
really worked out things that were alien/familiar to him. All of these, and
other figureheads, who would be at the table in a séance, would feel the
presence of the moment rising and falling like bodies turned into worms,
and as they put their hands on the Ouija board, they would realize they
were not part of any cause and effect moment except for what they would
be able to gasp of the coming together of east and west.

Well, so much for that. It's interesting to note that in HD's movement of the jellyfish as a lower bodily stratum moving up into the head, she senses this as the signal moment, and this is done way before her re-involvement with the Hermetic Brotherhood or who the fuck Mithras whatever, it is the elemental rising up from the sweet fish into the head. I mean this is also a great re-appraisal of Sappho's intelligence and, as she says, it's not for everyone. I've seen people pass out from the smell over here in Chinatown it gets pretty intense. But that orgy of life-form and what it derives from as it moves into the head is a powerful moment in the art.

RP: My project has been an arduous one as it heads off the map. I'm going for the back of the image, back of the word, back of abyss of reason. The fine line between magick and the poem dissolves and then I'm left with a hybrid and not sure what it can be called at that point.

Speaking of Richter and the image sans production and outside influence attached are a few pics here in response to 3 monsters. I do a lot of exploring in the hills and mountains as well as in my poetry. I constantly go off trail and find all sorts of odd places, and spaces. This rock recently revealed itself to me and spoke of monstrum, etc., so these images I give you in response to the seen monsters.

This one is very interesting as it remains hidden to most, was a real bushwack to get to. You'll have to visit sometime and I'll take you out into the middle of fucking nowhere to some very odd and remote backsides of the hills. Enjoy 3 views of reptile crag as I call it for now.

SD: Very fucking interesting. I have something in my notebook last day before getting kind of ill and in bed all day last day at the shore before flight home. I quickly wrote re what you are at here, *from* as opposed to *to*. It is in the ruins we visited (shit, still so many to see, that they've reconstructed everywhere it's really alot of earth working everywhere) but the whole thing is in the 'decorations.' I'll send a pic attached but they are sitting, all of those decorations (these residencies) in the woods or in the ground. There is a rotting as well as the soil giving out trees in the middle of the rubble which has designs after 1000 years held on the face of the stones etc.

So I wrote about thesis anti-thesis and also the idea of fugue in composing as echo to these cities, these ruins, these 'alphabets' is what they are. The decorations are patterns of bird feather, wing, serpent, etc, but they are designs and they go out from the structure, the residence or temple—they adorn in order to go out into the air and into the surrounding which is the place they pick up their circulation of interactive emanation. To read the words, letters, numbers, designs, decorations, all of them go out into space but into not just space it's the backside as you say of nothing. Which is a way of saying that reaching what is rusting and rotting and IS NOT THE DESIGN is the design too: a perfect enclosure for all movement, all living throw. Every element DOES THIS.

RP: Well, I knew there was a reason, or non-reason I was compelled to respond to your three monsters as after sitting with the poem as long as I had while you were away I was then compelled to re-sit with *Wandering.* Lo and behold everything that I had been missing dawned on me. Rather, what I had resisted I finally submitted to it and the final

poem, which is turning in to a serial poem, I sent you for it, "The
Concealing Voice" ruptured my placid complacency. I was just plain
accepting what I was writing without working it through clearly, the
basis for it that is.

So, in very rough form, from journals and IM chats with a longtime
friend, I'm attaching a little set of paragraphs to illustrate the genesis
of what I'm forced to call, and be called out by, "Exposure from the
Unexplored". The elimination of the choice to use 'from' instead of 'to'
was the all-deciding factor that I let do the choosing for me. Whatever
it may render see what you think.

For me, the whole thing spells massive relief. I knew I was missing
something and then to have it hit me square in the mind was an
incredible moment. The primary thing for me is that it moves me
beyond the concern for verbal expression of the poetic and carries it
forward through my magickal and meditative praxes. I could ramble
on about it, but I will leave off for now and let it stand as is for the
time being.

This whole process of wrapping up *Wandering* and exchanging notions
with you has been quite fortuitous. Your explorations in Mexico and
mine here may have coincided along certain parallel lines of some
strange synch. Will be interested to hear of any things that may have
come to you while on your trip.

Double-Wanded
Doubling
Dub
Δ

The act of doubling   As in back-gammon,
back, as in qliphothic tunnels running   once you double yr wager the
through yr back, or the totemic grizzly   next move to double is out of yr
circling back on you—look out   hands, not just a gamble for
                                                          some form of lucre, but
                                                          for the power to choose.
                          Like Mallarme's dice, it moves your hand-to-guts-to-
                          mind, except this cube can only move up and the
                          players may know its potential even if the risk is not so
                          clear.

Double-wanded, a poetics stands better as a writ for living than merely pen to paper writing.

Double-wanded actions: peculiar stylus inscribing the poet's world and slate, whether it be on the shell's
surface or at the core is a choice <again a double issue> as it cuts the crystal of the
macrocosm   this cube again   (the 30th æthyr and Crowley)

The nature of the nib   **and fount**

We say that we write in a "hand."
John Dee Δ wrote in several hands, one for
the queen, another for less formal correspondences,
and a scribble script for his magical diaries. He knew
the importance of codes, and the more recondite the
more he makes us toil for it. As Pound told us,
it can take some work to read poetry that is worth any
salt. The glyph and its proportions are part of the
body that send rays forth.

The ink of choice for grimoires—
dragon's blood, "they put their
souls into it...took blood sweat
and tears." Always a fluid, or
vital essence, soul/anima/animate
giving life to the work, the great
work,   "the first step to under-
taking the great work is hard
work." Proprioception is a vital
appropriation.

If "the pen is mightier than the sword" then that is why
roman scribes were not permitted to carry the bronze tri-form (epee'-like) stylus used for inscribing
upon the wax tryptych at the senate after Julius Caesar's death. Double utility. Writing for and writing
on the heads of state has its protocol and ultimately endows the poet with the pointedly aimless power
of usurpation—the route of poetic legislation as Shelley thought.

We've only tough hard substance to work out of now thanks to
Dee, Chapman, Williams, Lorca, Olson, and the like.

Signatura: revealing the magical script stamped (on Dante's substantial wax) inside everything
—at all times—songs waiting to be sung. And the concealment itself is a signing worth singing, contra-
puntal

Aphorism IV

Whatever exists by action emits spherically upon the

various parts of the universe rays which, in their own

manner, fill the whole universe. Wherefore every place

in the universe contains rays of all the things that have

active existence.

Dee's signature—emblem for his part in memoirs recounting dialogues: Δ for d or

fire, "the blue triangle is the ascending tongue of prayer" but for

fire, Dee's was red "the descending tongue of grace";

maybe it was just the hexagram hidden in a pointed tooth.

"Plunge from the height, O Man, and interlock with Beast!"

In THE WAY TO SUCCEED—AND THE WAY TO SUCK EGGS 69,

Aleister Crowley set it out:

This Interchange the Double Gift of Tongues, the word of Double

Power—ABRAHADABRA!—is the sign of the GREAT

WORK, for the GREAT WORK is accomplished in Silence.

And behold is not that Word equal to Cheth, that is Cancer

whose Sigil is ♋ ?

This Work also eats up itself, accomplishes its own end, nourishes

the worker, leaves no seed, is perfect in itself.

Little children, love one another!

And as this lies in <u>The Book of Lies</u> let's dismember that gammon, besides signifying a hind-quarter section of ham or bacon, was originally part of thieves' slang: "to keep in gammon" or seize someone's attention specifically with chatter, bruhaha or ridiculous nonsense; while a partner goes about robbing them. The art of deceiving fools or suckers—those who suck seed let's suppose.

      Being sucked in by the attractive eye-catching stuff in a piece of writing— Glitterati on the search—but then something in the periphery or seemingly less significant aspect of the poem causes a chain reaction of ideas and inspires the mouth. Reading aloud that feeds the ear.

But thieves as agents of Mercury don't deceive themselves, and only wish to steel our attention for a wile.

So we're going for the poet's duty to tongulate the listener's soul. The work yields a two-fold product: the poet is auditus and chanter, feels the connection and is audience, whereat the two fold into one, <u>back</u> to the monad. The poet sends forth and receives his double, as Shelley described, to digest its reports and feed the composition of magical verse. Anne Conway would say that this is a most modern and ancient movement. Linger in prolonged immersion will-devils! Is this the demi-**urge;** we've got to wonder with the Gnostic god-word for the *all*, ABRASAX, ABRAXAS, ABRAHADABRA to remind us that some gods men made were formed to roll off the tongue beautifully and hypnogogically.

     § Us poets may have our-selves in check, or rather **gammon**, concerning our

       deities, and the double momentum of the game is what gets us in tune, tones

the mind-muscle of our verse, and in the fury forget to make it work—our work, the balneum]

       our water, for drinking, bathing, and **swimming** in §

The freedom to forget is the core of repose—allows the dark spot in the mind to dub in the divine, sparks, wit, whatever you will when the time is right to re-member

Istorics/

Intuitive historiography

Blevins: "...Timing is everything"

Lansing: "analeptic, against time's"

Wilde:"It is part of that complex movement towards freedom which may be described as
the revolt against authority."

ACTIVELY ENGAGING HISTORY IS KERYGMA

What now at the Back-Game?

The most important thing about gaming, gamming–poetic self-deception, or playing from
the back is to keep it fun (let's go with Bob Black and destroy work as our government
forces it).

Poems can never be revised, only rewritten and this can be dangerous because of what
might be lost.

> To add on more stuff in revising—dub—doubling out
> those thoughts and those words are still there for the poet,
> put back of the addenda in digestion

Dubbing, the act of layering as in the recording studio, not the subtraction or cutting of
sound but its addition and thickening. Voice in the act of reading out-loud can do this en-
tirely.

All re- and un- doings are done   Or as I have long suspected we all have our
by the opposite hand of the initial act.   double being who treads the

For me it is the left, sinistra
palm that does it, the devil's {double}
hand that divvies up the extras.

mirror turf. Sight in the feet; leap up at us!

Finally at the Back-game. And for poetry, the written kind, the idea of gaming is most apropos.
Live it, then get it all down on paper taking care to maintain the integrity of the moment—this is
the <u>object</u> and not only a mirroring of it. As in the back-game everything is reversed putting one-
self on the defensive purposefully. Playing in the back-field as Duncan was often wont to do.

Image of the Mage painting a picture of the Magician developing a picture of the artist
ad infinitum. There is only so much that can be gleaned from achieving a detached
point of perspective when the object of our vision is the appearing world.
It is only when we seize the time to dwell on our shadow life—the dark mirror—that
we may understand the blackness that moves our puppet plays.

Austin Osman Spare's key—to slip into the back depths with a sigil,
a meaningless sign to all except the dwellers on the
threshold giving birth to the magical wish. Another
way of establishing a dialogue with that dark spot.

However, the further back we let
ourselves slip, the less control and
hence the need for an automatic
art as both Yeates and Spare rec-
ognized. The idea of hyper-text is
an old one, see Blake. Energized
enthusiasm is just another name for
the fidget babes with a purpose.

135

Plummeting deeper and
deeper till the necessity dissi-
pates, and the more we can pull
down with us the less need there
is for pencil and paper which is
evident in the colors and strokes
given to us by Falorio, Seaton,
Carrington, Clark Ashton Smith,
A. O. S. and all those who have
worked to render the latent im-
mediate on canvas.

The twenty-two tunnels of Set or quilpothic cells which Crowley unlocked again are keys to the
vacua of force and form. For the poet, this back-side or shadow of the tree of life is the fount
which provides the phantasmic mirror of mind with its mercury. Sandwiched between the vit-
reous and aqueous crystalline spirit it flows and circulates—a dredge.

The dance we gravitate to is at
"in-betweenness"
loc-us somewhere
twixt
Hellish roots
and
The Heavenly Tree

The model of the platonic cave may provide a doctrine and an impetus to drive, but let's leave
the moral overtones awash.

The poet's corpus
a meeting place is our duel duty
to wreak havoc with the wall—sustaining fabric

II

<u>Apophatic</u>

From Plotinus, Dionysius the Areopagite,
Crowley, and many others comes the method
of pairing an affirmation with its immediate
negation. Brings us closer to perceiving the
highest through the act of reading or chanting.

> No poststructural trickery, it doesn't
> dissolve into itself but hopefully we
> may dissolve in working out the
> apophasis

Nicholas of Cusa in his <u>Of Learned Ignorance</u> spoke of the coincidence of opposites as the
only way of approximating with words in describing the way things really are, much like
Parmenides wanted when he expressed his distrust of speech because we need words that will
signify a notion and its opposite simultaneously.

> Hamlet: To be or not to be
>> Let's drift in one step further and do both in act and thought:
>>> **BE NAUGHT!**

Apophatic   is to work towards the anagogic as Dante described in his letter to Can Grande

To be apophatic is to be apophis-like   just look at the sign of Apophis
                                                the destroyer, the two poles on
                                                     either side of the trident
                                                     all unite

                                                in mutual repulsion and attraction
                                                is how we become receptive
                                                (ie, set up our antenna).

▼

Amphibious logos, respiration, aspiration

the breath / word of those who live on both sides

All of the gill slits in man have been surpressed except for the first,

the ear opening, hence the pleasure of inhaling fluid sounds.

Every good poet seeks for the moments when their work flows, menstruum like, inspiration strumming their chords binding and locking their guts into the work. And we often find inspiration in the works that have flowed out of others—we **swim** on their blood. Immersion and submersion are obviously different—the real difficulty is how deep must we go. As deep as we allow meanings to penetrate us. The feeling is there like the primeval **swim** to unite with the egg, the poet learns the currents into Kali's flow that **swims** and overwhelms our senses—we must **swim** into the depths with abandon recording all we have found!

S P U Y T E N   D U Y V I L
Meeting Eyes Bindery
Triton
Lithic Scatter

TRACK   Norman Finkelstein

TRANSITORY   Jane Augustine

TRANSPARENCIES LIFTED FROM NOON   Chris Glomski

TRIPLE CROWN SONNETS   Jeffrey Cyphers Wright

TSIM-TSUM   Marc Estrin

TWELVE CIRCLES   Yuri Andrukhovych

VIENNA ØØ   Eugene K. Garber

UNCENSORED SONGS FOR SAM ABRAMS   (ed.) John Roche

UP FISH CREEK ROAD   David Matlin

VENICE IS FOR CATS   Nava Renek & Ethel Renek

WARP SPASM   Basil King

WATCHFULNESS   Peter O'Leary

WATCH THE DOORS AS THEY CLOSE   Karen Lillis

WALKING AFTER MIDNIGHT   Bill Kushner

WANDERING ELECTRON   Lee Slonimsky

WEST OF WEST END   Peter Freund

WHEN THE GODS COME HOME TO ROOST   Marc Estrin

WHIRLIGIG   Christopher Salerno

WHITE, CHRISTIAN   Christopher Stoddard

WINTER LETTERS   Vasyl Makhno

WITHIN THE SPACE BETWEEN   Stacy Cartledge

A WORLD OF NOTHING BUT NATIONS   Tod Thilleman

A WORLD OF NOTHING BUT SELF-INFLICTION   Tod Thilleman

WANDERING ON COURSE   Robert Podgurski

WRECKAGE OF REASON   (ed.) Nava Renek

WRECKAGE OF REASON 2 :

　　　　　BACK TO THE DRAWING BOARD   (ed.) Nava Renek

XIAN DYAD   Jason Price Everett

The YELLOW HOUSE   Robin Behn

YOU, ME, AND THE INSECTS   Barbara Henning

Made in the USA
Monee, IL
07 July 2026

56549088R00092